MW01234055

# Izzy Iguana Climbs a Tree

## A Geometry Book

Written by Jacqueline Williams
Illustrated by Jolie Gray

Copyright © 2020 Jacqueline Williams
All rights reserved
First Edition

PAGE PUBLISHING, INC.
Conneaut Lake, PA

First originally published by Page Publishing 2020

ISBN 978-1-64628-775-8 (pbk)
ISBN 978-1-64628-776-5 (digital)

Printed in the United States of America

For Isabella

I am Izzy's tree.

I am Izzy.

Every day, I climb up the trunk of my tree.
The trunk has **parallel** lines.
**Parallel** lines are two lines that are always
the same distance apart and never touch.
Can you find the parallel lines in the trunk?

Sometimes I stop to admire the view. When I look up, I see lots of branches to climb on. The branches **intersect** each other.

**Intersecting** lines are lines that share exactly one point. The shared point is called the point of intersection.

Can you find the intersecting lines?

I like to crawl from one end on a branch and go as far as I can go. Sometimes I crawl fast, and sometimes I crawl slow. I like the branches that are like a straight **line** and have no curves, especially when I crawl fast!

A **line** in geometry is a straight figure that extends infinitely in both directions.

Can you find the straight figure that is a line?

If I climb too high, as I sometimes do, my mom says, "Little Izzy, you're climbing too high!"

She only wants me to climb to a certain **point** on the tree. But I like to climb!

A **point** in geometry is an exact location. A point is shown by a dot.

Have you ever climbed too high in a tree?

Sometimes it gets a little tricky climbing on my tree. Sometimes branches break, and there is only a small part to crawl on. That's when I crawl really slow from the trunk to the end of the branch. If I crawl too fast, I might fall off this **segment** of the tree.

A **line segment** is a piece, or part, of a line in geometry. It is represented by a point on each end of the line segment.

Can you find the line segment?

When I finally crawl down from my tree, my mom is always waiting! She stands up on her back legs, and I do too. We hold out our front legs and say, "Gee, I'm a tree!"

She likes that I have learned geometry!

## About the Author

Jacqueline Williams is a retired teacher who lives with her husband Mark and cat Cleo in Alabama. She has always enjoyed reading with her children, students, and grandchildren! Her love of reading, encouraged by her mother, and her love of teaching inspired her to write and spread a love of learning!

CPSIA information can be obtained
at www.ICGtesting.com
Printed in the USA
LVHW070126080520
655013LV00004B/157

9 781646 287758